A God's Dream

25 blessings learned in 25 years

XIOMARA HECHAVARRIA

met·a·mor·pho·sis

/ˌmedəˈmôrfəsəs/

Noun

A change of the form or nature of a thing or person into a completely different one, by natural or supernatural means.

To the collective,

Know that this book isn't only for souls making their 25th lap around the sun. This is for all ages to reflect and help find the hidden blessings in your life. I'm hoping to be the light that guides you into awakening. I dedicate this book to my family and friends because you all have inspired me to be the higher me.

Table of Contents

Chapter 1: Above 1

Chapter 2: 222 2

Chapter 3: In Tune 4

Chapter 4: L O V E 6

Chapter 555 - Ascension 7

Chapter 6: Surrender 9

Chapter 7: Prayer | Manifestations 11

Chapter 8: Journaling 13

Chapter 9: Faith over Fear 17

Chapter 10: Mental Wealth 19

Chapter 11:11 21

Chapter 12: Want vs. Need 23

Chapter 13: Single Szn 25

Chapter 14: Ex-factor 27

Chapter 15: Know your worth 29

Chapter 16: Gratitude 31

Chapter 17: Yin and Yang 32

Chapter 18: Financial Diet.. 33

Chapter 19: Everything is Everything... 35

Chapter 20:20 Vision 36

Chapter 21: Passion & Purpose 37

Chapter 22: We meet again Love 38

Chapter 23: Birds of a Feather 40

Chapter 24: Family.. 42

Chapter 25: Metamorphosis 45

Chapter 1: Above

God is good all the time, and all the time, God is good. In the last 25 years of my life, I've experienced many lessons, and in this book, I'll take you through them. But to get started, it wouldn't feel right to not give my immediate thanks to God. To me, God is everything. Both God and the universe are interchangeable, and being able to acknowledge this allows my soul to tap into the abundance surrounding us. Knowing the God in you is the key importance to having the life you deserve. A God's dream is a culmination of love, self-confidence, inspiration, vibration, frequency, and the all-knowing. His blessings are readily available, tap in!

"These days, I'm letting God handle everything above me."

- H.E.R.

Chapter 2: 222

While I have abundance on your mind, let's talk about synchronicities or what I like to call: A kiss from the universe. The 222 angel number has to do with balance, and manifesting timely miracles. Above all else, it reminds you that you're in the right place at the right time. That's a blessing in and of itself, right? So let's dive deeper into that. Keeping your balance will allow you to stay focused. Too much of anything is never good, so maybe you see 222 when you're indulging too much into your desires, or you're not giving yourself enough love. It can be a combination of things, but when you see that number, know that you are in the right place at the right time and it's time to modify your energy.

October 13th, 2019

"222, I've been seeing you everywhere, especially when I least expect it. I know you're here to give me a sign, and I appreciate you for being there. To my guides, I love you, I hear you, and I thank you. Let's handle this life and do it damn good! And then do it even better in the next one. From me to you, 222."

Chapter 3: In Tune

I want to address this topic early because to receive these messages to your core, you have to be in tune with who you are. In case no one has told you today, you are a spiritual being having a human body experience.

Being spiritual doesn't necessarily mean you're religious. By practicing spirituality you become aware of who you are and <u>you align yourself to be in tune with your highest self</u>. Two practices that help me stay in tune are setting intentions and trusting my intuition. Those two factors alone will keep you in the awareness frequency, which in turn will keep you in tune. I also enjoy lighting incense and listening to music to help me stay connected. Figure out what keeps you aligned and incorporate it in your daily routine. You will know when you're disconnected because that's where ego, fear, and hate live.

Alignment happens more often than not for me. When I tell you I'm a different person than I was yesterday.. I mean it. Most of the time I can have an improved way of thinking within an hour. When I do something out of character my highest self gets me in check real quick. This is such an important part of spirituality because a lot of people think spirituality is all happiness and being naive when in reality you are constantly going through uncomfortable realizations. Which leads me to the blessing that comes from being in tune: *Sense of self.* Developing a sense of self will lead you to your values, goals and ideals which are all apart of your highest self.

PSA: Gaining *spiritual happiness* should be one of the most important goals in your life.

Chapter 4: L O V E

That four-letter word. Is it too early to get deep? You're right, it is. We'll circle back.

But above all else, **Love is Love.**

Chapter 555 - Ascension

Ascension is the process of elevating your energy and awareness into new worlds of perception, experience, and creation. Going from one layer to the next, so to speak. You can ascend within a dimensional reality (energy plane or "world")as well as between dimensions.

In 2017, I experienced my first symptoms of ascension, which aren't like your normal body aches but rather chakra pains, ear ringing, and, most importantly, the need to go inward for answers. This is when I first tapped into my higher self and was able to visualize my future. Ascending is not easy, and for some readers, this will sound intangible… which is why I'm happy you're here. Ascending in spirituality is the expansion of consciousness. It goes by other names like Spiritual Awakening or Enlightenment. If you haven't already, at some point, you will ask yourself, "What is life?" When you're actually ready to tap into that question, you will begin to ascend. Let go and allow your soul to ascend through this dimension because that freedom will allow you to surrender and fully live the God's dream.

cue "Ascension" by Maxwell

Chapter 6: Surrender

How does one surrender?

By surrendering to life, to your guides and trusting your instincts, you will be liberated into your truth. Let go of control by allowing yourself to open up fully and surrender to positive communication.

In society now, we imagine the worst-case scenario, and that's depressing. Deconstruct your subconscious. Our mind and emotions can hold us back from our dreams. Imagine what it feels like when you're at the happiest moment in your life. Go deep into that focus and feel into the emotions of it. Open the gateway because thoughts become things. Something will happen today that will change your life for the better… if you're ready for it.

Here's my daily surrender practice: Close your eyes, unclench your jaw, drop your shoulders and release your tongue from the top of your mouth. Become one with your surroundings and feel into the energy that surrounds you. Maybe it's a light breeze on your skin, the smell of fresh-cut grass, or maybe a new candle. That feeling of peace is surrendering, now in that moment tap into the abundance that surrounds you.

Chapter 7: Prayer | Manifestations

A lot of people are waking up to their powers so it's only right to make this known. Do not replace prayer with manifesting. Prayer is key; prayer is vital to receiving any of the blessings God set for your life. When you pray, you let God know you are ready for what he has for you. I pray so much it's gotten to a point where I speak to God in public. Remember the surrendering we talked about before? Prayer is the perfect practice. We need silence to hear God speaking in our hearts. Praying is setting the tone to speak something in existence, and that's where manifestations come in.

Manifesting is fairly simple, but it's solely based on trust. If you have a vision and you know in your heart it'll happen then you don't need to know how, why or when. As long as you know it's yours because you claimed it, then it's yours. However there's one vital part to manifestations that a lot of people tend to forget. To achieve your dreams you still need to do the work. This is not Aladdin and the Will Smith genie is not popping out the lamp. Get clear on what you want, get to work and trust that it's yours.

The last step I'd recommend if you're looking to truly manifest your future is to write it down. No matter how outlandish or crazy you think it may be, write it down. Journaling is a hobby I use as an outlet for multiple things, but it's an amazing feeling to read your journal at the end of the year and see what you've accomplished. Do what you need to do to make your dreams come true because you don't want to get to the end of your life wishing you did more.

Chapter 8: Journaling

Habakkuk 2:2-3

King James Version

[2] And the Lord answered me, and said, Write the vision, and make it plain upon tables, that he may run that readeth it.

[3] For the vision is yet for an appointed time, but at the end it shall speak, and not lie: though it tarry, wait for it; because it will surely come, it will not tarry.

Journaling is so powerful because everything you went through that year is documented, and your story matters. Never forget where you came from, but in that same breath, be excited about where you're going.

I'm going to insert a few dated journal entries I've written over the past few years. These entries will give you an idea of how I manifest, acknowledge the light and dark, and always stay grateful. You will notice parts of my journal that speak in third person, and this happens during my writing when I know God takes over. This is a new level of vulnerability; however, since you're reading this, I would love nothing more than to share with you.

February 18th, 2018.

A few days ago, I broke down into tears because I felt overwhelmed with the Lord's love. I could feel his warmth in my body. I asked him to help me with all my confusion and feelings, and I'm writing today to say he has. The love of the Lord is an indescribable feeling. I'm here to manifest a few things because my mind is running out of space for my ambition.

Security. Stability. Health. Love. Success.

This is your world, Xiomara, do with it what you want. But be happy while doing it. You have amazing things coming to you. I need to know you'll be grateful for them all. Welcome to your new chapter.

April 6th, 2018

I'm happily here to say that I bought my big girl car last month! I'm beginning to realize the sort of powers I have. Last month I paid off all my debt, then got my car, and received an internship at a public relations firm and got promoted at work. I am so grateful for this beautiful universe encompassing me with love. Thank you, Lord, for being my best friend, I will remain on your path and remain faithful because you have not proved me wrong since. I love you. Gratitude is my essential attitude.

April 7th, 2018

I've been going through these weird periods where I can't help but have negative thoughts. This is a defense mechanism that I use when I'm heartbroken. If I remain in full faith, there's no reason to be scared or upset.

Remain in a positive frequency. Negativity will try to come into your life, but overshadow it with positivity because seeing another day is good enough. You are good enough.

March 22, 2020

Well, here I am, God. I am here with all of the chaos going on in the world right now. I'm thankful to be surrounded by souls that uplift me. Being stuck in quarantine is the perfect time to reassess, reset, realign, and do anything you've been wanting to do. For the first time yesterday, I stayed in my bed all day, and I loved it. The air feels much easier to breathe. The trees are growing and flourishing. Lord, please bless humanity and allow us to come out of this healthy, in love and safe.

Chapter 9: Faith over Fear

You know the saying, "It's easier said than done"? That's how replacing fear with faith works. It's easier to sit in a state of fear, but it isn't practical in order to survive. Fear is not only a negative frequency, but it's almost always out of an irrational state. For example, let's say you hate flying. The pilot tells the cabin you're 44,000 feet up in the air, and then you begin to hit turbulence. Your fear kicks in, and you visualize the plane falling out of the sky, and you didn't even get to tell someone you loved them first. The way I've dealt with this is a simple mantra, "Faith over Anxiety, Hope over Worry and Love over Fear." Repeat this to yourself until you feel better. Use this mantra in any situation that scares you, because God has you, but only if you truly believe that.

More than overcoming fear, have faith in yourself. Know your truth, and have faith in your ability to accomplish anything. Read that again.

Leave with this prayer: Lord, I love you. I thank you for keeping my loved ones safe. I ask that you protect me from what does not serve me. You have truly blessed me with so much abundance, and fear is holding me back from being truly grateful. Amen.

Chapter 10: Mental Wealth

Our brains are the most powerful muscle in our body, and most people struggle with delegating that power. Two years ago, I was in the best shape of my life from constantly staying active and using a new women's pre workout. For the first time in my life, I could feel my heart beating out of my chest, and that feeling created anxiety. Nights would go by, and my anxiety would increase until I was able to figure out the problem being the pre-workout which wasn't FDA approved (which is almost all of them, so be careful). I remember an instance of me being so anxious on a plane that I ended up grabbing my neighbor's hand and squeezing it so tight. He took his headphones off and asked, "Are you okay?" I was so nervous I couldn't even respond. He looked at me and said, "It's just turbulence, don't worry, but I think you may have anxiety. Here's a trick that I use when I'm anxious" and he proceeded to calm me down. I'll never forget that moment because, in an uncharted experience of true anxiety, God had someone there to help me. If you or someone you know deals with anxiety or mental health issues, remember we all have struggles. In case you didn't know, there are hidden blessings in anxiety. *Empathy and personal discovery.* When you realize you're anxious, you have the ability to do the inner work to calm your mind. Even if you don't get anxious, learn to be there as a calming soul that empathizes for someone who does.

So while people are out here working on their mental wealth, be the random neighbor that keeps them grounded even when they're 44,000 feet in the air.

Chapter 11:11

It's currently July 11th, 11:11am PST

Five years ago, I became a barista because I was a broke college student who needed to pay rent and the coffee shop was within walking distance from my house. Sometimes I even used to take my brother's car (Sorry, Miguel, but these Vegas summers are no joke). I remember working early mornings, so stressed to make ends meet, but it was such a valuable part of my journey. Well, today, I am sitting in that exact coffee shop writing my first book.

While working in this exact establishment, I used to visualize myself in a better position, living a comfortable life, and following my dreams. Well, five years later, I can confidently say, "I made it, and I'm here." We all measure success differently but my hope for you is that you always know your value is internal. I never for once doubted my ability to be in the position I'm in today, and I hope you never doubt yours either.

Do you hear that? **That's inevitability.**

Chapter 12: Want vs. Need

What is it that you want? - Scratch that.

What does your soul need?

The answer is found in the deepest level of awareness and compassion that you generate when you gently strip down all of your layers.

Acknowledge the…

- -dedication
- -vulnerability
- -confusion
- -creativity
- -passion

Remove the...

- -external attachments
- -irrational ideas

Appreciate the…

- -authenticity of each moment

If I've learned anything from my spirituality journey it's the ability to differentiate between what I want from what I need. Gratitude has helped me refrain from the desires I "want" because I'm happy for everything I have. Being grateful also let's God know you'll appreciate more of the blessings given to you along the way.

Example: You may want a relationship because everyone on Facebook is getting married. But when you remove the external attachment to other people's happiness you may realize you're not even ready to give someone all of your time right now. When you ask yourself what you need, know that the answer will always be <u>you</u>!

Chapter 13: Single Szn

The pivotal point in your life where you can just be... What is it about being single that is so confusing yet so liberating? So envious yet so mysterious. I'm at a point in my life where I don't know where I'm going, and it's hard to reflect on where I was, but I can find so much happiness where I'm at.

I've been so prepared in my single szn that I've even made lists to describe my "perfect" man. Shortly after reading *Relationship Goals* by Mike Todd, I realized I needed to rip up those lists. All I can do is be the person I want to attract.

Before the person, I asked God to help me stay on the path of discovery. To be able to distinguish what's right for me and become the woman that I deserve to be. Take time to figure out who you are while single. Because if you don't, you'll pick someone based on what you think you want, not who you truly deserve. No one wants to spend the rest of their life translating their heart to someone.

I'm currently single because my heart is inspired by a multidimensional love, and in order to reach that, I had to develop a few things in myself.

- Character
- Work Ethic
- Emotional Health
- A better relationship with God

In my mid-twenties, I've managed to reach my purpose without someone, and I hope you've found that too. Relationships don't improve singleness; it exposes it. So with that being said, become the person you want to be with. All else will fall into place, trust.

Chapter 14: Ex-factor

To love or not to love? That is the question.

Always choose love. But if you choose to love an ex again... just remember that whatever reason made you exes in the first place meant your bond was breakable. It's imperative for me to acknowledge how impactful my different experiences with love were. I've been blessed to know a lot of different versions of love even the unhealthy ones. I've learned that you can't take what people say at face value, you have to let them prove everything to you. However, it didn't matter who broke whose heart but rather the hidden blessing that comes from relationships. That blessing is *forgiveness*. Self-forgiveness allows you to release the need to be perfect or feel guilty about a decision you've made. Second, forgive the others that may have taken advantage of your vulnerability.

Remember that everyone is on this earth to fulfill a certain destiny. Heartbreaks will hurt but do your best to not take anything personally. Let the forgiveness of God live inside of you because we all deserve that level of peace in our life.

Lastly, learn from your history, be selective with your energy and do not confuse longevity with being meant to be.

Proverbs 4:23

Above all else, guard your heart,

For everything you do flows from it.

Chapter 15: Know your worth

Knowing your worth isn't just a consideration or a possibility; knowing your worth is the bare minimum before any relationship you enter. You won't tolerate anything that doesn't serve you if you know your worth. Work hard, provide yourself with the things that make you happy. Don't trip over the half-ass friendships and relationships that were no good for your soul anyway; only be grateful for the ones that are.

I'm convinced no one is worth your time until they prove to you otherwise and I don't mean this in an egotistical way but truly think about it. Behind closed doors you're doing the work, learning from your mistakes and figuring out your strengths and weaknesses. Don't let just anyone have access to your soul because unless they've done the internal work they won't know how to value you.

Your value doesn't decrease based on someone's inability to see your worth. Just from opening your heart to receive the messages from *A God's Dream*, your price has already gone up... now add tax.

Chapter 16: Gratitude

I'll keep it simple, baby.

Gratitude is the key.

Chapter 17: Yin and Yang

The principle of Yin and Yang is that all things exist as inseparable and contradictory opposites. For example, dark-light and old-young. I wanted to touch on the dualism of life because you cannot have one without the other. This book has presented so many ways to tap into positivity, love, and happiness but the reality is life is HARD and we'll all experience fear, negativity and pain. With spirituality comes awareness and the all-knowing. Remove the naive characteristic from your soul because trials and tribulations are inevitable.

What I want for you to do is remember how temporary feelings are. No matter how bad things get there's always going to be a better day. When you find yourself in a dark place, remember the God in you. Take some rain with your sunshine and tap back into God's dream.

Chapter 18: Financial Diet

It's amazing to me how many of us sit in classrooms for years and then have to teach ourselves about the importance of financial freedom. My parents were reluctant enough to give my brother and I everything we wanted. That mindset didn't make me greedy, but instead helped instill a positive idea towards money. I see currency as energy. Similar to anything else, you give it, and it comes back. But if you try to hold onto it, then you're in the mentality of lacking... and that's what will eventually happen.

If you haven't already, start studying financial literacy. There's plenty of information and diagrams that let you know exactly how to budget every month. I managed to pay off debt, build my credit and buy a new car off of a hostess wage. It's definitely possible.

It's easy to get caught up buying the material things in life, because honestly, shopping online is my jam. But I've learned saving money is a priority because it's better to pay yourself for your hard work instead of paying Zara or Louis Vuitton. Don't get me wrong; if there's something you love, give it 72 hours, and if you still want to purchase it, I support it. (Don't quote me, though, because I don't want to be the reason anyone goes broke.)

Allocate your expenses, save your coins and no matter what, always secure your own bag.

Chapter 19: Everything is Everything

The next time someone asks you "how you are," respond with "Everything is Everything." This may sound vague, but to the right ears, it will make sense. "Everything is Everything" means everything is going according to plan. My life was written before I was born, and I came into this world to fulfill my destiny and so did you. Life is going to continue to happen whether we want it to or not; all we can do is choose how we react and handle situations. The only thing that remains the same is change and knowing that should keep you on your toes. We're not put on earth to remain stagnant and comfortable but rather to experience and love ourselves enough to always make a better situation. You're exactly where you need to be.. it's all about living in the moment.

Chapter 20:20 Vision

The year is 2020, and the world is finally brought with uncomfortable conversations about racism, inequality, and hate. Oh yeah, there is also a pandemic, natural catastrophes, and men and women being killed because of the color of their skin. This all sounds insane, right? Well, my friends, welcome to the awakening. If you are not tired then you aren't paying enough attention. It pains me to see human beings treated like they're less than all over the world. Do not wait until it affects you personally to care because this is OUR problem as the collective consciousness. The hidden blessing amidst the chaos is that injustice is finally getting enough coverage. We owe it to the next generations to keep fighting for a better day.

"So when we're marching and protesting and posting about the Michael Brown Jr's and Tatiana Jefferson's of the world .. tell your friends to pull up."- Rihanna

Chapter 21: Passion & Purpose

With "everything going on," I never let myself tap into the fear or propaganda presented by our media because the constant negativity affects my frequency. This level of awareness allowed me to see my path much more clearly, and I truly came into my passion. I'm passionate about finding light in the midst of darkness, and my purpose is to share those learnings with the collective also known as *A God's Dream*. It took me 25 years to truly figure out what made my heart happy, and I'm honored to be sharing that moment with you right now.

There comes great power when you're able to connect your passion and purpose. There is something God made about you that is meant to make a lasting impact in this world. If you're unsure on where to look, I'd first recommend that you starve your distractions. Maybe even take it to the next level and implement fasting for 21 days. Once you apply pressure you'll inevitably get closer to God and that level of clarity will fuel your passion. *You are the hidden blessing, act accordingly.*

Chapter 22: We meet again Love

I told you we'd circle back, so here we are.

By now, you have an idea of the versions of love I've experienced, but it wouldn't be fair if I didn't tell you the hidden blessing in love... which is *Creation.*

Personally, I love being a spiritual creator, voila the book in your hands today. Our parents are creators; thanks, moms and dads. It is *love* that moved God to create because he loved life so much he was moved to create characters to share this love. Love is a reformer and a teacher. It will make someone unrecognizable and change them for the better. A lot of people would even consider love to be the strongest drug of them all. If I may make a request... do not take love for granted because happiness is not something we buy; it has to be created.

One of my favorite hobbies is to sit in a public place and look out into spaces and watch people fall in love with each other. There's no doubt that I'll meet my other whole and experience something so deep and intimate, but that's on God's time. I'm content knowing I love my family, my friends, and most of all, myself. Self-love is the best love because it lets people know how to love you. In the wise words of Jhene Aiko, "I love me enough for the both of us."

1 Corinthians 13:4-8

[4] Love is patient, love is kind. It does not envy, it does not boast, it is not proud. [5] It does not dishonor others, it is not self-seeking, it is not easily angered, it keeps no record of wrongs. [6] Love does not delight in evil but rejoices with the truth. [7] It always protects, always trusts, always hopes, always perseveres.

[8] Love never fails.

Chapter 23: Birds of a Feather

I've come across some amazing souls in my life, especially the ones I met on the bus in 6th grade. When you're young, the people you meet unintentionally shape your personality and the experiences play a role in who you will inevitably become. I was blessed to have met some of the souls of my lifetime. When I was young, my parents used to tell me I wouldn't even remember my childhood friends once I went to college. On the contrary, God's managed to keep those people closer to me than some of my college friends.

When people show themselves to you, you have to believe them. If they're a good person, keep them close. If they show you any part of them that compromises the integrity of your peace? To the left, to the left.

I'm in a long-distance friendship with the majority of my friends but I have all the tools to keep them thriving. I mean, who's going to tell my future husband I already have about 12 soulmates? There's a handful of people that knew I was taking the journey to share *A God's Dream* with the world and gave me nothing but endless love and support. I love you all so much, and I thank you for being my family.

S/o to Cleveland, Ohio, and Las Vegas, Nevada for giving me some forever memories. I'd flock together with you all any day.

Chapter 24: Family

For me, the importance of family came with my age. It's not that I don't have a big family, because it's quite the opposite, but I moved around enough to where that connection became distant. It's important for me to touch on this topic because I would not be the woman I am today without my family. I come from a family of hard-working, strong individuals, and I knew from a young age that I would not let their hard work go to waste.

My father comes from immigrant parents that set out to live a better life, but in that same breath, his life wasn't easy either. It's interesting to hear my father's life stories because he came from little to nothing and provided me with everything. I will not let that go unnoticed, and my kids will know where they came from.

My mother is the most caring soul I've ever met. You know the type to ask, "Do you want a snack?" You respond, "No," and she brings it anyway? That's my mama. My mother didn't have it easy either, and she has overcome many adversities, all to become the beautiful strong woman she is today.

My brother has been with me from day one, and even though I used to tell people he was adopted (he's not). Miguel constantly inspires me to keep my head held high. He is an inspiration because life doesn't come easy to a gay black man, and he is crushing life, rightfully so.

Lastly, I want to thank my grandmothers. The coolest women in the game. They say most traits skip a generation, and I can feel that to my core. Mi abuela in Honduras is where I get my most caring traits from. She's transferred to me the power to make the best out of any situation. Te amo, Mika. Then there's my incense loving, no meat eating, yoga practicing gram; she inspires me so deeply. I could be walking down the street, and she'll be sure to say, "You are so great at walking, you can do it for a living." No matter what, she constantly supports my every move.

Now that you have a glimpse at where I came from, I want to acknowledge the family members of mine that aren't blood related. My family has brought so many people into my life that have either inadvertently or intentionally shaped me into the woman I am today and I couldn't be more thankful.

What I hope you take from this chapter is that *blessings are generational*. We not only owe it to ourselves to set the tone for the future, but it's also a way to salute the path in the past. There's no words to accurately convey how grateful I am for all of my family that has paved the way for me. I know you're all reading this… You are my biggest blessing. I love you.

Chapter 25: Metamorphosis

When I was about five years old, I had a caterpillar tree in front of my house. I would play with caterpillars all day long not even realizing as they got older, their lives would completely change into something much more beautiful. 20 years later, I see butterflies everywhere, and I know it's not only a sign from God but symbolism of my own life. The metamorphosis stage of a butterfly signifies growth, adaptation, and beauty. Spiritual growth and transformation can only occur in your life when you finally sit still and stop moving. With all of the blessings in my life it feels like this is my second time doing everything, and I've finally unlocked the matrix.

The hidden blessing from *A God's Dream* is being able to share this metamorphosis with you all because I am a reflection of you.

My name is Xiomara Hechavarria and I am an Afro-Latina woman, now author, who is honored to be sharing her story with you. I've experienced an immense amount of internal growth and blessings over the past 25 years and I can confidently say I now have my wings.

Above all, you keep your clarity

You keep your focus

You keep your sense of love

And you keep your sense of purpose

Those are, they're integral, you know they're key

Happiness, you know ...

A lot of people define success differently

For me, you can have everything, all the money in the world

But if it's not enjoyable, if it's not sustainable

If you can't be a person of integrity while having all of these things

What does it matter? What does it mean?

The value is internal,

Your value is internal

Lauryn Hill

Made in the USA
Monee, IL
06 September 2020